Recipes to accompany
Port Wine

by
Hélio Loureiro

Translated from the Portuguese by
Magdalena Gorrell Guimaraens

3

FISH DISHES

MEAT DISHES

DESSERTS

In Portugal, one is assisting to a curious contradiction regarding Port Wine. On the one hand, it is increasingly praised by critics who do their utmost to make it known, albeit sometimes in a rather erudite manner that is beyond the reach of the majority of its consumers. On the other hand, no matter how much the public at large strives to follow this trend, there are relatively few opportunities for opening a bottle of Port and consequently, consumption tends to be limited to more festive occasions such as Christmas and Easter. Unfortunately, people are not greatly accustomed to appreciating the multiple varieties of this beverage with meals, something which would make it possible for this magnificent product to be better known and savoured by all. One must also bear in mind that there have been many, somewhat violent, attempts to get people to drink Port with meals. Over-zealous *aficionados* have even gone to the extent to organise entire meals around this fortified wine. In my opinion, this is absolute nonsense as, as everyone knows, Port is a wine that is fortified with grape spirits and has an alcoholic content of around 20°. I would not recommend a banquet where the amount of alcohol actually drunk would be doubled, which would be the case were Port to be drunk throughout instead of the so-called calm wines. The use of Port is something that ought to be carefully thought out, with a view to serving a specific dish of the several that are on the menu. This is the fundamental purpose of this book. Therefore, this is not a compendium of select recipes that have been bound to be given to our guests during an immense feast accompanied solely by Port Wine, with the sole purpose of showing off our knowledge and grasp of wine. The real object of this book is to make it possible for a host to serve, either at the beginning, in the middle or at the end of the meal, a Port that has been carefully chosen to accompany a particular recipe.

This book is a collection of recipes ranging from hors d'oeuvres to desserts, salads, pasta, meat and fish dishes. From now on, only he who does not wish to do so, will not lack in opportunities to drink the forgotten bottles of Port stored in a corner of his winecellar.

Great care was taken in selecting a wine range of white, ruby and tawny Ports, as well as special category Ports. This was entrusted to a team consisting of João Nicolau de Almeida, Miguel

Castro Silva and myself, who tasted the dishes that were created by Chef Hélio Loureiro. We tackled this task by first examining each recipe on paper and then trying to guess, in a rather abstract manner, just which was the most appropriate wine. Interestingly enough, we were pleased to discover, as we tried out the dishes, that we had gotten practically each one right. One must not forget that there is always a subjective component to a tasting which is why, in this book, we only make suggestions as to which wine we recommend. Furthermore and most important, it must not even cross the reader's mind that the advice that is given herein in any way reflects the opinion of the Port Wine Institute, or anything remotely like that! This is purely a report of suggestions that we all agreed with and that we felt were the most appropriate.

What were our criteria? Imagine, for a moment, that you are sitting with us and asked to give your opinion. First of all, we must consider our memory, those events which are stored in our brains and that reflect earlier tastings of the product. Should this mental tool fail us, we can also count on the possibility of bringing ourselves up-to-date by tasting the numerous samples of this wine placed at our disposal by the Port Wine Institute. Thus we taste them all, over and over again, commenting on our impressions until we establish a set of parameters with which everyone is in agreement. Once this transcendental step is taken, together we examine the recipe. There are a set of factors that will govern our choice: texture, predominant taste, use of sauces, presence of vinegar, spices, behaviour of the ingredients, manner by which it is cooked, aromatic herbs, etc. To do so we attempt to create an image that is closest to the sensation created by each recipe. Thus, for a delicate dish, we will look for a wine with the same characteristics, one that is older and more complex, with tertiary nuances; still, in the case of a stewed partridge, for example, where the flavours are sharper, we will have to decide upon a more robust, a younger Port, one full of primary aromas. You see, it is not so complicated an affair.

Generally speaking, the younger the red wines, the more full-bodied, the greater the structure, with more tannins and a greater predominance of ripe fruit; these are ideal for spicier dishes. Aged tawnies, on the other hand, have developed in wood and lost the exuberance of the fruit and the tannins, yet they have acquired an elegance and a complexity of aromas of dried fruit, iodine, *vinagrinho*, exotic woods, balms, etc.; more tamed than younger wines, it is theoretically easier to combine them with food. Regarding the white Ports, there are two fundamental features that must be considered: their degree of sweetness and their age, given that some aged white Ports are more like tawnies in terms of their golden brown colour and the wealth of their aromas.

What appears evident is that practically all dishes can be accompanied by Port Wine, as long as it has been carefully selected in light of the recipe and the rest of the meal. I believe that this is the great purpose of this book: to abolish the myth that Port is a luxury product, that it must be kept in the winecellar, that it is only a dessert wine, and to make Port work for us. Should we have been successful, we will all have gained from this as we shall be able to delight in, more diligently, one of the finest wines in the world, one which, perhaps because it is so close to hand, does not receive the merit is deserves. Let us, then, lift our voices on behalf of this prodigal son of Portuguese gastronomy and raise our glasses to our next feast: To Port Wine!

Alfredo Hervías y Mendizábal

TYPES OF PORT WINE

Only wine produced in the Douro Demarcated Region under strictly controlled standards of production and ageing is entitled to the denomination of Port Wine.

Throughout the ageing process, the wine is subject to analytic and sensorial quality control tests carried out in the laboratories and by the panel of tasters of the Port Wine Institute (IVP), one of the oldest and most distinguished public entities in Portugal. The principal mission of the Port Wine Institute is the official ontrol and the defense of the prestige of Port Wine and to promote this product world wide. Only those wines who comply with the strict criteria for quality set by the IVP are authorised to bear this entity's seal of guarantee.

White Ports

As indicated by their name, these wines are made solely from white grapes, mainly the following varietes: Malvasia Fina, Donzelinho, Gouveio, Codega and Rabigato.

White Ports have a varying degree of sweetness, from the very sweet so-called Lagrima, to the Sweet, Semi-Dry, Dry and even Extra Dry. Their alcohol content is usually between 19% vol. and 22% vol. There is a special category called Light Dry that, in addition to being quite dry, present an alcohol content of 16.5%.

Red Ports

There are two great groups in the family of Red Ports: Undated Ports (Ruby, Tawny, 10, 20, 30 and More than 40 years old) and Dated Ports (Vintage, LBV and Colheita).

Several grape varieties are used for these wines, most especiallly: Touriga Nacional, Tinta Amarela, Tinta Barroca, Tinta Roriz, Touriga Francesa and Tinto Cão.

Undated Ports

These are blended wines whose originality resides in the delicacy with which they have been blended. These are not simple wines; they are works of art that result from the careful mixing of up to fifteen different types of wines from different years. Their bouquet and harmony are obtained through a controlled oxidation as they mature in wood.

When they are young, these wines are subjected to several transfers at a rate and number that will vary according to the techniques and winemaking style of each shipper and determine the manner by which they will develop as they age. Once bottled, Undated Port Wine is ready for drinking as its characteristics will not change significantly should it remain in bottle.

- Ruby – This is a blended wine whose deep red colour reminds one of the precious stone of the same name. This is a young, full-bodied and fruity red wine obtained by blending wines of different harvests.

- Vintage Character – Results from the blending of superior quality Ports with an average age of between three and four years. Containing a complex structure, it is noted for its body and intense fruit.

- Tawny – Takes its name from the English word that describes its colour. Tawny is obtained from blending wines that have aged in oak casks. These wines age more quickly than Ruby. As the wine oxidises, little by little its colour acquires slightly orange, tawny hues. With average 3 years of age, these wines are elegant and delicate.

- Tawny With an Indication of Age – 10, 20, 30 and More than 40 Years Old Tawnies represent blends of wines from different years that have matured in wood and whose average age is the one indicated on the label. Their golden colour comes from prolonged ageing in wood. The principal characteristics of these Ports are the complexity of their aromas, their fresh taste, persistant bouquet and elegance.

Dated Ports

This group marks the difference between Port Wines that are aged in wood and those which, after spending a relatively short period in wood, are left to age in bottle.

• Vintage – Vintage is truly precious. After spending two years in contact with wood, it then ages slowly in bottle away from air and light. Little by little, the characteristics of the wine develop considerably and it acquires its bouquet. The label, in addition to indicating the year in which it was made, must indicate the year in which the wine was bottled. This category includes the so-called Quinta Vintages which are wines made from the grapes grown solely on the estate whose name they bear on the label.

Considering that these wines may be drunk in the years after they have been bottled, they should be allowed to age in bottle. With time, the wine will throw a deposit and therefore it must be carefully decanted before serving. As these wines begin to age in bottle they have an intense deep purple colour and their aromas are very complex, very fruity and floral. As they age the colour of the wine changes and all its harmony and complexity become more striking.

• LBV (Late Bottled Vintage) – This extremely fine quality wine is made from grapes harvested solely in the year indicated on the label. Before it is bottled, LBV spends 4 to 6 years in wood to age, during which time its colour develops more quickly than Vintage. These wines have a very intense colour, are full of tannins, young in nature, and with a slightly oxidative component to their bouquet that is a result of their initial aging in wood.

• Colheita – This is Port Wine made from grapes harvested solely in the year which is indicated on the label. These wines age in wood and are only bottled just before they are placed on the market. They are a minimum of 7 years old which gives them a golden colour and a taste that is smooth, delicate, profound and complex.

Starters

Cheese Soufflé

from S. Jorge Island in the Azores

grated Ilhas cheese	200 g
flour	60 g
hot milk	$^{1}/_{2}$ litre
eggs	4
savory herbs	to taste
butter	60 g

Heat the butter and add the flour all at once, add the previously grated cheese, the savoury herbs, the hot milk and simmer for about 10 minutes.

Separate the yolks of the eggs and add to the above mixture, after it has cooled slightly. Beat the egg whites stiff and fold in gently.

Butter individual soufflé molds and half-fill with the above mixture.
Cook at 200°C in a pre-heated oven for 20 minutes.
Remove carefully from the oven and place on a napkin, on a plate.

Serve with a salad seasoned with olive oil, raspberry vinegar,
salt and pepper.

Note: Ilhas is a sharp, Cheddar-like cheese from the Azores

4 to 6-year-old LBV

Duck Salad

garnished with a salad of lettuce greens, apples and cider vinaigrette

duck breasts	240 g
Cooking oil	1 dl
seed bread	200 g
cider vinegar	to taste
virgin olive oil	as required
apples	100 g
butter	25 g
sugar	30 g

Season the breast of duck with salt and black pepper. Heat the cooking oil in a frying pan and when it it hot, brown the breast of duck. When it begins to gain colour, place in the oven for 10 minutes.

Slice the breast of duck and sauté it again in the fat left in the pan until it is toasty.

In a bowl place the lettuce greens and season with salt, pepper, olive oil and cider vinegar. Chop the apple into small cubes and sauté in hot butter. Add sugar and cook until golden. Sprinkle over the lettuce.

Serve the well-toasted slices of breast of duck on a bed of salad. Garnish with toasted bread croutons.

Ruby or Vintage Character

Breaded Pig's Ear

with a fresh mushroom salad

pig's ear	250 g
breadcrumbs	100 g
egg	1
fresh mushrooms	200 g
lettuce	250 g
tomatoes	100 g
cooking oil	2 dl
virgin olive oil	1 dl
balsamic vinegar	1 dl

Cook the pig's ear until tender in water seasoned with salt, black pepper
and bay leaf. Cool, drain and slice into strips about 1 inch wide.
Dredge in egg, flour and breadcrumbs. Refrigerate for 1 hour, then fry.

Meanwhile, cut the mushrooms into thin slices and season with salt,
pepper, olive oil, vinegar and the tomatoes cut into cubes.
Set aside for a few minutes.

On a serving platter, arrange a bed of lettuce sliced into thin strips, cover
with the seasoned mushrooms and place the breaded pigs' ear on top.

Vintage Character or Young LBV

Salt Cod Salad

pressed, with fresh coriander, tomatoes and marinated capiscum

salt cod	250 g
onion	100 g
garlic clove	1
tomatoes	200 g
capiscum/bell peppers	150 g
unleavened corn bread	250 g
chopped black olives	100 g
olive oil	1 dl
black pepper	to taste
fresh coriander	to taste

Shred the dry salt cod and put to soak in cold water, changing the water often. Season with olive oil, vinegar and black pepper. Cut part of the onions into thin slices, chop half the garlic and mix well with the cod. Press the mixture into muffin tins and refrigerate.

Broil the peppers, peel, cut into thin slices and season with olive oil, pepper and salt.

In a small pan, heat the olive oil, add finely chopped onions and garlic and the tomato, cut into small cubes. Simmer gently and season with salt and pepper. Add the finely chopped fresh coriander.

Place a small amount of the tomato sauce on a serving platter, arrange the sliced peppers and place the unmoulded cod salad in the middle. Garnish with chopped coriander, black pepper and chopped black olives.

Serve with fried slices of unleavened corn bread.

10-year-old LBV

Stuffed Tomatoes

with fresh cheese and smoked salmon

tomatoes	4
fresh cheese	250 g
smoked salmon	200 g.
sliced toast	4
oregano	to taste

Slice the top off the tomatoes and remove the flesh, taking care not to pierce the bottom or the skin. Season inside with salt and pepper.

Cut the smoked salmon into small strips, season with lemon juice and black pepper. Mix with fresh cheese cut into small cubes. Toss with salt, vinegar and olive oil.

Fill the tomatoes and garnish with chopped parsley.

4 to 6-year-old Tawny or Special Reserve

Fresh Water Fish Fillets

with raisin bread and onion marmelade

fresh river fish (trout, carp, eels)	400 g
onions	200 g
fresh bread dough	400 g
egg	1
flour	to taste
raisins	50 g
red current jam	40 g
red wine	1 dl
lemon	1
cooking oil	1 dl
mustard	1 Tbsp.
herbs from Provence	1 packet
Chopped parsley	to taste

To make the raisin bread, knead the raisins into the bread dough. Sprinkle flour on the table and make a roll about 15 inches long, brush with the beaten egg and cook for 25 minutes at 200°C in a pre-heated oven. The bread is cooked when a toothpick is inserted and comes out clean. Cool, slice and toast.

To make the onion marmelade, chop the onions and place in a pot with the red wine, red current jam and mustard. Boil until almost all the liquid has been reduced.

Gut and clean the fish carefully and cut into small fillets, taking care to remove all the bones. Season with lemon juice, salt and black pepper. Dredge in flour and fry in hot oil. Remove excess fat by draining on a piece of paper towel.

Place the slices of toasted raisin bread on a serving platter. Arrange the onion marmelade and the fish fillets. Garnish with chopped parsley and mixed herbs.

4 to 7-year-old Tawny

Prawns in Batter

and deep-fried vegetables with a tomato and country herb sauce

raw prawns	800 g
string beans	200 g
small squashes	200 g
carrots	200 g
flour	150 g
eggs	3
beer	1.5 dl
peeled tomato	200 g
onion	1 medium
garlic clove	1
country herbs	to taste
olive oil	as required
cooking oil	as required
fresh coriander	chopped
fresh parsley	chopped

Blend flour with egg yolks, beer, sal, pepper and a trickle of olive oil.
Mix well. Beat egg whites until stiff and fold in the mixture.

Cook the vegetables and slice lengthwise, dip them in the batter and
fry in hot oil. Drain on paper towel. Keep warm.

Shell the prawns and season with salt and black pepper.
Dip in batter and fry in hot oil, as for the vegetables.

Heat the olive oil in a frying pan, add finely chopped garlic and onion,
peeled tomato cut into small cubes, let boil and season with salt and pepper.

On a serving platter, pour the warm tomato sauce,
arrange shrip and vetegables,

Season with black pepper and garnish with chopped fresh
coriander and parsley.

20 or 30 Years Old Tawny or corresponding Colheita

Molded Poultry Mousse

with nutmeats and corn bread

chicken	250 g
partridge	1
onions	2 medium
almonds	25 g
raisins	25 g
walnuts	25 g
olive oil	1 dl
foie gras	50 g
garlic clove	1
pitted black olives	50 g
butter	1 Tbsp
thyme	to taste
sheets of gelatine	20
raspberry vinegar	to taste
olive oil	to taste
corn bread	toasted slices

Cook the chicken and the partridge in water seasoned with salt and pepper. Cool, remove from the bones and shred.

In a pan place the olive oil, onion, chopped garlic and bay leaves. Add shredded poultry and simmer for some minutes. Place into a meat strainer and purée. Soften the sheets of gelatin in gold water and add to the puréed poultry (warm the purée slightly so that the gelatine will dissolve properly).

Line individual moulds with cling film and fill with the mousse. Refrigerate approximately 3 hours.

Melt a tablespoon of butter in a frying pan, add roughly chopped nutmeats and sauté until golden.

Place a layer of nutmeats and lettuce leaves seasoned with salt, pepper, raspberry vinegar and olive oil on a serving platter. Unmould the mousse and place a slice of foie gras over each. Garnish with slices of toasted corn bread and sliced, pitted olives.

10 to 15-year-old LBV

Melon Soup

with mint leaves and aniseed bread

fresh bread dough	200 g
aniseed	to taste
egg medium-sized	1
honeydew melon	1
mint leaves	to taste
dry wine	2 dl

Kneed the bread dough with the aniseeds and let rise in a warm place.
Bake at 200°C in a pre-heated oven for approximately 20 minutes. The
bread is cooked when a toothpick inserted in the center comes out clean.
Remove from oven, cool and slice. Place again in oven to toast slightly.

Meanwhile, open the melon, remove the seeds and peel.
With an electric mixer, mash the melon and add the dry wine.

Serve the soup in cups garnished with mint leaves and accompanied
by slices of the toasted bread.

Semi-dry White

Cheese Mille-feuilles

with fresh cheese and thin slices of smoked ham

flaky pastry	200 g
cured Serra cheese	40 g
fresh cheese	200 g
Smoked ham	200 g
lettuce leaves	to garnish

Roll the flaky pastry out thinly and sprinkle with the grated, cured Serra cheese. Pre-heat the oven to 250°C. Bake for 10 minutes, reduce the temperature to 150°C and bake another 15 minutes.

Cut the cooked pastry into small rectangles 6 inches long and 2 inches wide.

Cut the pastry in half lengthwise and fill with slices of fresh cheese and smoked ham.

On a serving platter, sprinkle a trickle of olive oil mixed with a little Sherry vinegar and season with salt and black pepper. Arrange the slices of mille-feuilles in the centre and garnish with lettuce leaves.

Ruby or Vintage Character

Salad of Breasts

of quail sautéed in olive oil and raspberry vinegar

quail	4
mixed salad greens	300 g
cubed carrots	100 g
toasted almonds	40 g
olive oil	1 dl
Raspberry vinegar	1 dl
cubed apples	to garnish
Cooking oil	1 dl

Remove the breasts from the quail and season with salt
and black pepper.
Remove the bones from the legs and season with salt and black pepper.
Sauté all the meat in hot oil and reserve.

Make a sauce with the ground toasted almonds, olive oil and
raspberry vinegar, seasoned with salt and pepper.

Toss the salad greens with the cubed carrots, season with the sauce
and arrange on a serving platter. Place the breasts on top,
together with the shredded meat from the legs.

Garnish with toasted almonds and small apple cubes.

20 Years Old Tawny or Semi-sweet White

Fried Black Rice

sausage with potato and apple salad on sautéed white cabbage

black rice sausage from Leiria	200g
cooked unpeeled potatoes	150 g
white cabbage	200 g
cooking oil	1 dl
apples	150 g
olive oil	1 dl
white wine	1 dl
mustard	1 tsp

Slice the cabbage leaves into thin strips and simmer gently for 5 minutes In white wine with 50 g of apples cut into cubes, mustard, salt and pepper. Cool and place on the bottom of the serving platter.

Fry the sausage or, if you prefer, bake for a few minutes until crispy.

Slice the remaining apples, unpeeled, into half circles. Sauté in butter and a little oil. Peel the cooked potatoes, slice into half circles, add and sauté until brown.

Toss the apples and potatoes with the sausage and serve on the bed of sautéed cabbage.

Young LBV or 10 to15-year-old Vintage

Breast of Chicken

stuffed with Mirandela sausage on a bed of fresh pasta

chicken breasts	4
Mirandela sausages	2
fresh fettucine	180 g
fresh mushrooms	100 g
finely sliced carrots	100 g
thick cream	2 dl
Butter	25 g

Remove the skin from the chicken breasts and slice them lengthwise.
Bake the Mirandela sausage and remove the skin.

Stuff the chicken breasts with the sausage meat. Wrap the chicken
breasts in cling film and roll tightly to form little sausage rolls.
Steam for 10 minutes or, if you do not have a steamer, place in a pan
in a bowl of water, cover and cook in a low oven for 20 minutes.
Cool before removing the cling film.

Meanwhile, boil the fresh pasta in water seasoned with salt and pepper.
Drain, adjust the seasoning and add a trickle of olive oil

Slice the mushrooms and carrots into fine strips and sauté quickly
In very hot olive oil. Toss with the fresh pasta.

Slice the chicken sausage roll and serve on a bed of the fresh pasta.

20 or 30-year-old Vintage or 10 to 15-year-old LBV

Salad of Sea Shells

sautéed with tomato and onion and accompanied by a crusty sesame seed pastry

large sea shells	8
onions	2
flaky pastry	250 g
peeled tomato	1 can
garlic clove	1
egg	1
olive oil	1 dl
sesame seeds	20 g
chopped	parsley
fresh fennel	garnish

Wash the sea shells well and boil in lots of salted water for 2 hours.
Cool, remove the meat and cut into small cubes. Heat the oil in a frying
pan. Add chopped garlic and onion and the cubed peeled tomato.
Simmer for a few minutes, add the shell meat, stir and
adjust the seasoning.

Meanwhile, roll out the pastry, cut in half and sprinkle one half with the
fennel and sesame seeds. Cover with the other half and roll again.
Cut four 2 x 15 inch rectangles, brush with beaten egg and bake
in a very hot oven for approximately 15 minutes until done.

Separate the pastry in half lengthwise, place the shell meat and cover
with the other half of the pastry.
Season with black pepper and garnish with chopped parsley and fennel.

10 Years Old Tawny

Salad

of grilled cuttle fish with vinaigrette sauce on a bed of fresh pasta

cuttlefish	400 g
onion	1 medium
fresh noodles	200 g
thick cream	2 dl
garlic cloves	2
olive oil	2 dl
red wine vinegar	1 dl
fresh or dry oregano	to taste
Serra cheese (optional)	to taste

Clean and gut the cuttlefish, rinse and season with salt and pepper. After they have been grilled, slice in thin rings, season with chopped garlic olive oil and red wine vinegar.

Boil the fresh noodles, sauté them in the cream previously seasoned with salt, pepper and oregano.

Serve the sliced cuttlefish on the bed of fresh noodles. Garnish with fresh herbs and, if you wish, with cured Serra or Ilhas cheese.

Young Tawny or Sweet White

Fish Dishes

Fish Dishes Toasted

loin of monkfish with pine nuts and Julienne vegetables

loin fillets of monkfish	800 g
onion	1 medium
leeks	2
small squashes	100 g
carrots	100g
peppercorns	20
thick cream	2 dl
white wine	2 dl
butter	100 g
toasted pine nuts	40 g
soy sauce	to taste

Make butter sauce by heating the white wine, peppercorns, cubed onions and 1 sliced leek in a pan. Boil until all the wine has evaporated. Add thick cream and simmer until the amount of liquid is reduced by half. Remove from heat and add butter cut into small pieces. Beat well with a whisk.

Press the entire mixture through a sieve.

Season the fillets of monkfish with salt, pepper and lemon juice. Dredge in flour and fry in hot oil until golden. Place in an ovenproof dish and bake at 200°C for about 20 minutes.

Meanwhile, cut the carrots, squashes and the remaining leek in thin slices about $1/2$ inch across. Heat a little oil in a frying pan, add the vegetables and season with salt, black better and soy sauce. Sauté until done.

Arrange vegetables and monkfish on a serving platter and garnish with lightly toasted pine nuts. Serve with butter sauce.

20 to 30-year-old Tawny

Cod Pasty

with marinated red capsicum and crumbled corn bread

soaked salt cod	400 g
red capsicum/bell pepper	200 g
potatoes	4 medium
tomato	150 g
onions	2
crumbled corn bread	200 g
garlic cloves	2
egg yolk	1
Milk	1/2 l
olive oil	2 dl
bay leaf	1

Place equal quantities of milk and water in a pan with the bay leaf and 1 garlic clove and bring to a boil. Place the soaked salt cod in the water and remove immediately from the heat. Leave to poach for 20 minutes.

Meanwhile, wash the capsicum and broil, peel and cut into thin slices. In a frying pan, heat the olive oil and add the other garlic clove, the sliced onions, the sliced capsicum and the crumbled corn bread. Mix well.

Place a large metal ring, about 3 inches across (a cookie cutter will do) on the serving plate. Inside, place a layer of onion and crumble mixture, a layer of poached cod and another layer of the onion mixture. Crumble a little more corn bread, mix well with a beaten egg yolk and finish filling the ring. Place a few seconds under the grill.

Serve with cooked greens sautéed in olive oil and garlic, unpeeled boiled potatoes sautéed in very hot olive oil and seasoned with salt and black pepper.

10 to 15-year-old LBV

Fillets of Turbot

with crunchy almond pastry and capers sauce

fresh fillets of turbot	720 g
leeks	2
onion	1 medium
carrots	200g
string beans	200 g
egg whites	4
flour	100 g
chopped toasted almonds	100g
white wine	1/2 dl
thick cream	2 dl
butter	50 g
bay leaf	1
capers	to taste
thyme	to taste
fresh herbs	garnish

Season the fish with salt and pepper and set aside. Mix the finely chopped toasted almonds with the flour and egg whites. Knead well and roll out thinly. Bake until golden and well cooked. Cool and cut into small rectangles with a serrated knife. Dredge the fish and fry until golden in hot oil. Place in an ovenproof dish and bake until done.

Meanwhile, place the white wine, the onion, the sliced leeks and the bay leaf in a pan and boil until all the liquid has evaporated. Add the cream and reduce by half. Remove from the heat and add the butter in little pieces. Beat well with a wire whisk and add the capers. Cut the carrots and green beans into thin slices, sauté in butter and season with salt, pepper and thyme.

Place a slice of almond crocant on a serving plate, add the fish and the vegetables and top with another slice of almond pastry. Pour the butter sauce over the whole and garnish with fresh herbs.
Serve with sauté potatoes or saffron rice.

Young Tawny

Fresh Salmon

on a bed of onions and carrots with potatoes and apples

fresh salmon slices	800g
potatoes	600 g
carrots	200 g
onions	2 medium
fresh mushrooms	200 g
apples	2
olive oil	2 dl
flour	2 Tbsp
cooking oil	2 dl
thyme	garnish
chopped parsley	garnish

Peel the apples and the potatoes (but do not wash the potatoes).
Cut potatoes and apples into thin strips and mix.

Heat a little oil in a frying pan and fill with the potatoes and apples,
pressing down on them with a skimming ladle. Sauté until golden and
place in a hot oven for about 10 minutes. Remove from oven and cut
again into slices with a knife.

Season the salmon with salt and black pepper, dredge in flour and fry in
hot oil until golden. Place in an ovenproof dish and bake at 200°C for
10 minutes. Meanwhile, peel the carrots and wash the mushrooms.
Slice onions into thin half moons and simmer in a pan with a little oil.
Add carrots cut into thin sticks and mushrooms cut into quarters.
Cover and simmer, seasoning with thyme, salt and pepper.

Make a bed of vegetables on a serving platter.
Wrap the fish in the potato and apple strips and place on the vegetables.
Garnish with thyme and chopped parsley.

Young Tawny

Stuffed Sardines

with corn bread and crabmeat on a bed of mashed potatoes and crispy vegetables

large fresh sardines	8		corn bread	150 g
crab	1		tomato sauce	2 dl
onions	2		breadcrumbs	50 g
carrots	100 g		flour	50 g
leeks	100 g		lemon	1
small squash	100 g		olive oil	2 dl
eggplant	100g		cooking oil	2 dl
tomatoes	2 medium		bay leaf	2
garlic cloves	2		chopped parsley	garnish
eggs	2			

In a large pot of water seasoned with salt and pepper. Cut half an onion into cubes and half in slices and add. Bring to a boil and add crab. When it comes again to the boil, cook for 5 minutes. Cool and remove all the crabmeat. Heat the olive oil in a frying pan and add chopped onion and garlic, one bay leaf, the crumbled corn bread and the crab meat. Mix well.

Slice open the sardines, remove the bones and season with lemon juice, salt and pepper. Stuff the sardines with the seasoned crab meat. Dredge the sardines in flour, dip in the egg and then the breadcrumbs. Press tightly to close and fry in hot oil. Drain on a paper towel to remove excess fat.

Cook and mash the potatoes, adding milk, butter and one egg yolk. Slice the vegetables into thin strips and fry them in very hot oil. Drain. Place them in a hot oven to crisp.

On a serving dish, place a round of mashed potatoes (use a 3 inch diameter metal ring to shape it). Place the sardines and the crisped vegetables on top. Pour the tomato sauce around the whole. Garnish with chopped parsley and slices of lemon.

Young Tawny

Breaded Fillets of Hake

with hazlenuts and shrimp rice

fillets of hake	800 g
shrimp	400 g
flour	50 g
eggs	2
onions	2 medium
garlic cloves	2
rice	240 g
brandy	1 glass
white wine	1 glass
ground toasted hazlenuts	50 g
tabasco sauce	to taste
cooking oil	2 dl
olive oil	1 dl
bay leaves	2
sliced lemon	garnish
parsley	garnish

Shell the raw shrimp. Sauté in olive oil and garlic until golden. Remove the shrimp but keep the pan juices to which you add the chopped onion, bay leaves and the shells. Simmer then add a glass of brandy, bring to a boil and strain. Replace in pan, add a glass of white wine and bring to a boil. Add 3 glasses of water. Season and boil. Add rice, reduce the heat and cook for about 15 minutes.

Turn off the heat and add the shrimp. Rest for 5 minutes.

Season the hake with salt and black pepper. Dredge in flour, dip in egg and ground toasted hazlenuts. Fry in hot oil and drain well.

Make a bed of rice on a serving platter with the shrimp on top and then the breaded fish fillets. Garnish with ground toasted hazlenuts, slices of lemon and a sprig of parsley.

20 to 30 Years Old Tawny or corresponding Colheita

Sautéed Monkfish

with cherrystone clams and shrimp

monkfish	800 g
cockles/ cherrystone clams	400g
shrimp	400 g
potatoes	200 g
ripe tomatoes	2
onions	2
garlic cloves	2
white wine	1 dl
lemons	2
bay leaf	1
chopped parsley	to taste

Heat the olive oil in a pan, add the garlic and sliced onions and fry until golden. Add chopped tomatoes and simmer. Add the white wine and bring to a boil. Add the cockles/clams and cook until the shells open.

Cut the monkfish into 2 inch cubes and dredge in the flour.
Add the monkfish and the shelled shrimp to the above mixture, cover and cook for 10 minutes.

Serve with boiled parsley potatoes.

10 Years Old Tawny or corresponding Colheita

Crayfish Mille-feuilles

with shellfish sauce and small vegetables

crayfish	1200 g
fresh mushrooms	200 g
carrots	200 g
small squashes	200 g
onions	2 medium
garlic cloves	2
flaky pastry	200 g
egg	1
brandy	1 glass
white wine	1 glass
butter	2 Tbsp
flour	2 Tbsp

Roll the pastry out into 6 x 2 $\frac{1}{2}$ inch rectangles. Brush with beaten egg and bake at 250°C for 10 minutes. Reduce the heat and leave to dry for another 15 minutes. Cool, open in the middle and place the bottom half on a serving dish.

Shell the raw crayfish. In a pan, heat the olive oil and add the onions, 1 clove of garlic and bay leaf. Simmer for a while then add the shells and stir. Add the white wine and brandy. Add two level tablespoons of flour and stir well. Add two glasses of water and boil for another ten minutes. Sieve and beat well with a wire whisk. Just before serving, add two spoons of butter.

In a frying pan heat olive oil, 1 chopped clove of garlic and the vegetables cut into small cubes. Simmer a little and then add crayfish. Sauté altogether and season with lemon juice, black pepper and salt.

Place the crayfish on the pastry and pour the sauce overall.
Cover with the other pastry half.
Serve with white rice.

20 Years Old Tawny

Fillets of Cutlass Fish

on a bed of celeriac, leeks and potatoes

fillets of cutlass fish	800 g
celeriac	100 g
leeks	200 g
potatoes	400 g
flour	2 Tbsp
lemon	1
savoury herbs	to taste
chopped parsley	garnish

Season the fish with lemon juice, salt, pepper and savoury herbs.
Dredge in flour and fry in hot oil. Drain on a paper towel
to remove excess fat.

In a frying pan, heat olive oil and add finely-sliced celeriac, potatoes
cut into small cubes and sliced leeks.
Season with salt and pepper.

Make a bed of potatoes, leeks and celeriac.
Sprinkle with black pepper and chopped parsley.
Place the fish fillets on top and garnish with slices of lemon.

Young Tawny

Trout Stuffed

with green cabbage and pieces of smoked ham

trout	4
smoked ham	100 g
finely shredded green cabbage	200 g
potatoes	400 g
onion	1 medium
corn bread	100 g
bay leaf	1
lemons	2
olive oil	2 dl
chopped parsley	to taste
chives	to taste

Clean the fish and slice open along the backbone, taking care not to open the stomach. Remove the backbone and side bones, leaving the rest of the fish attached to the head and to the tail.
Season with salt, black pepper and lemon juice.

In a frying pan, heat the olive oil and add the garlic and chopped onion and simmer until golden. Wash and dry the shredded cabbage, crumble the corn bread and add both to the pan. Simmer for some minutes.
Cool and use this to stuff the trout.

Wrap the stuffed trout in aluminium foil and bake for approximately 15 minutes. Remove the foil with care and replace the fish in the oven to grill for a few minutes.
Meanwhile, boil the potatoes in their skins, peel and sauté in hot olive oil. Season with salt, pepper, chopped parsley and chives.

Make a bed with the potatoes and place the stuffed trout on top.
Garnish with chopped parsley and black pepper.

Vintage Character

Fresh Noodles

with shrimp and mussels

fresh noodles	240 g
shrimp	200 g
shelled mussels	400 g
onions	2 medium
garlic cloves	2
chopped peeled tomatoes	3
olive oil	1 dl
basil	to taste

Boil the fresh pasta in a large pot of salted water for 4 minutes.
Drain and set aside.

In a frying pan, heat olive oil and chopped garlic.
Add chopped onion and tomatoes.
Simmer for a few minutes. Add shelled shrimp and mussels.
Mix gently with the pasta and season with salt, pepper and basil.

Garnish with fresh basil.

❧

Dry White

Fillets of Sole

stuffed with freshwater shrimp in a rice chowder

sole	4
freshwater shrimp	400 g
rice	2 cups
onion	2 medium
garlic cloves	2
lemons	2
bay leaves	1 dl
tabasco sauce	to taste

Clean the sole, cut into fillets and season with lemon juice,
salt and black pepper.
Heat a large (at least 10 cups) pot of water seasoned with salt,
tabasco sauce and one quarter of an onion. When it comes to a boil,
add the shrimp. As soon as it comes again to a boil, remove from the heat
and spread the shrimp over the table to cool rapidly, then shell.
Set some shrimp aside for garnishing

In a large pan, heat the olive oil and add the garlic and onion.
Simmer well. Add 4 cups of the liquid in which the shrimp were cooked.
Add rice and cook slowly for 15 minutes. The rice should be soupy.

Meanwhile, in a small pot, melt 1 Tbsp of butter and add 1 Tbsp flour.
Mix well and cook a few minutes. Add one cup of the liquid in
which the shrimp were cooked and mix well.
Add the shelled shrimp.

Roll the fillets of sole around the shrimp. Dredge in flour and fry in hot
oil until golden. Bake for about 10 minutes.

In a deep dish, place the rice with its liquid and the rolled fillets of sole.
Garnish with the reserved shrimp and chopped parsley.

Tawny Reserve

Octopus

stewed in red wine and accompanied by sautéed potatoes

octopus	1200 g
potatoes	400 g
onions	2 medium
leeks	2
garlic cloves	2
red wine	2.5 dl
bay leaves	2
thyme	to taste
cornstarch	

In a pressure cooker, heat the olive oil, add the garlic and onion and
simmer. Add bay leaves and the raw octopus cut into thick slices.
Add red wine, stir, cover,
bring to a boil and cook for 10 minutes.

Boil the unpeeled potatoes, cool and cut into quarters. Add sliced leeks
and sauté in olive oil. Season with salt, pepper and thyme.

Thicken the wine sauce with a little cornstarch.

Make a bed of the potatoes and leeks and place the octopus on top.
Pour the wine sauce over all.

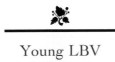

Young LBV

Stuffed Cuttlefish

mountain country style

cuttlefish	16 medium
mixed wheat and rye bread	100 g
mountain paprika sausage	40 g
country cured ham	40 g
onions	2 medium
garlic cloves	2
olive oil	2 dl
peeled tomato	200 g
cooked red kidney beans	200 g
red wine	1 dl

In a pot, heat half the olive oil and add the crushed garlic, one chopped onion and a bay leaf. Simmer a little and add the finely chopped chouriço sausage and cured ham (previously soaked in water to remove excess salt). Soak the bread in water, squeeze as dry as possible and add. Mix well.

Stuff the cuttlefish with the above mixture. Skewer with a toothpick to close them. Simmer together olive oil, garlic, onion, tomato and a little red wine. Add cuttlefish and cook until done. Add the cooked kidney beans and boil for 5 minutes.

Remove the toothpicks from the cuttlefish and replace in the pan.

Serve with slices of toasted mixed wheat and rye country bread.

20 year-old Vintage

Baked Black Grouper

with marinated dry vegetables in the style of Goa

For the vegetables		For the fish	
capsicum/bell peppers	200 g	grouper/jewfish	1200 g
carrots	100 g	onions	2 medium
cawliflower	100 g.	lemon	1
string beans	100 g	breadcrumbs	25 g
mustard seed	1 Tbsp	ground almonds	25 g
sugar	2 Tbsp	salt and pepper	to taste
chopped dry chili peppers	1 level tsp	olive oil	4 Tbsp
ground cumin	1 heaping tsp	mashed potatoes	
freshly ground ginger	1 tsp		
wine vinegar			

Slice the vegetables into thin strips and place in salted water for 24 hours.
Drain and dry well with a cloth.
Place to dry in the sun for several hours or in a 50°C oven.

Mix the vegetable spices. In a frying pan, heat a little oil and add the spices,
the vegetables and a trickle of wine vinegar.
Cover and simmer for 15 minutes.

Clean the fish and slice it into small slices. Season with lemon juice, salt
and pepper. Slice an onion and place in an ovenproof dish.
Place the fish on top and sprinkle with ground almonds and breadcrumbs.
Pour a tablespoon of olive oil over each slice and bake in at 200°C
in a pre-heated oven for 15 minutes.

Place the fish on a bed of vegetables and garnish with parsley.
Serve with mashed potatoes.

10 to 15-year-old LBV

Meat Dishes

Breaded Lamb Chops

with timbales of carrots, spinach and mushrooms

lamb chops	20	thick cream	1 dl
breadcrumbs	as required	white wine	1 glass
eggs	3	butter	as required
flour	2 Tbsp	cooking oil	as required
carrots	200g	red capsicum	1
cooked spinach	200 g	mint	1 sprig
fresh mushrooms	200g	black pepper	to taste

Season the lamb chops with a little white wine, salt and pepper.
Dredge in flour, dip in egg and breadcrumbs and set aside.
Fry only just before serving.

Boil and mash the carrots. Add 2 eggs and 1 dl of cream. Season with
salt and pepper. Place in buttered individual aluminium molds, place in
a pan of water and bake at 200°C for 15 minutes.

Meanwhile, chop the cooked spinach and sauté in the remaining cream,
seasoned with salt and pepper.

Slice the mushrooms and sauté in hot olive oil seasoned with salt
and pepper.

On a serving dish, place the chopped spinach, the carrots moulds
and the sautéed mushrooms. Place the freshly fried lamb chops
and garnish with slices of lemon and a sprig of mint.

Old White or 10 to 20 Years Old Tawny

Partridge

with hot vegetable relish

partridges	2
onions	3
carrots	100 g
potatoes	400 g
1 red + 1 green capsicum	2
garlic cloves	2
white wine	2 dl
wine vinegar	1 dl
bay leaf	2
olive oil	2 dl
gorse	1 sprig
rosemary	1 tsp

After cleaning the birds, season with salt, pepper, white wine, 1 bay leaf
and a sprig of gorse. Marinate for several hours.

In a pan heat half of the olive oil and add the garlic, thinly sliced onions
and 1 bay leaf. Fry until slightly browned and add carrots
cut into very thin strips.
Cook a little longer and set aside.

Sauté the birds until golden in the remaining olive oil. Cover the pan
and simmer over a low heat for 45 minutes or until tender.

Place the cooked onions in a frying pan and cook at a high heat. Season
with salt and pepper. Add the remaining white wine and the vinegar.
Bring to a boil and pour over the cooked partridges.

Boil the unpeeled potatoes. Cool slightly, peel and sauté in olive oil
and a little rosemary.

Young Vintage

Sliced Veal Tenderloin

with "punched" potatoes and red wine vinegar and oregano sauce

tenderloin of veal	800 g
coarse salt	to taste
potatoes	8 small
onions	8 small
raw chestnuts	200 g
red wine vinegar	1 glass
butter	1 Tbsp
milk	1 Tbsp
olive oil	2 dl
oregano	to taste

Make a sauce by mixing the oregano, olive oil and vinegar.

Sprinkle the potatoes with coarse salt and bake about 20 minutes in a 200°C oven. When cooked, remove excess salt and punch down lightly to crack them open.

Season the meat with coarse salt and pepper. Grill over very hot charcoal and cut into thick slices.

Meanwhile, shell, boil and purée the chestnuts, adding a little butter and milk.

Cut the onions in quarters and cook in very hot olive oil. Season with salt.

Make a bed with the chestnut purée and place the meat and onions on it. Arrange the potatoes around the meat. Pour a little of the sauce over and serve the rest on the side.

4 to 6-year-old LBV

Small Tenderloins of Pork

wrapped in flaky pastry with herbs on a bed of white cabbage and beans

small tenderloins of pork	800 g
white cabbage	600 g
dry scarlet runner beans	200g
flaky pastry	200 g
onion	1 medium
egg	1
olive oil	2 dl
sesame seeds	to taste
fresh thyme	chopped
fresh rosemary	chopped

Season the pork with salt and black pepper and brown in hot oil.
Drain off all fat.

Roll out the pastry and sprinkle chopped herbs over it. Wrap around
each pork tenderloin and brush with beaten egg. Place on a flat oven
sheet in a 250°C oven.
Cook for 5 minutes and reduce heat to 150°C and cook 10 minutes more.
Slice with a sharp knife when done.

Meanwhile, heat the olive oil in a frying pan and add sliced onion.
Wash and drain the cabbage and shred in thin strips. Add to the pan
and sauté lightly. Add previously cooked beans, cover and cook
a little longer until the cabbage is done.

Make a bed of cabbage and beans on a serving dish and place
the sliced pork on top.
Garnish with chopped herbs and sesame seeds.

20 to 30-year-old Vintage

Pheasant Stuffed
with foie gras and dry mushrooms

pheasants	4		Port	1 glass
foie gras	150 g		red wine	2 dl
dry mushrooms	100 g		lard small amount	
onions	2 medium		cravinho	
potatoes	12 very small		star flower anis	to taste
onions	8 very small		cloves	to taste
peeled raw chestnuts	150 g.		rosemary	to taste
sliced smoked bacon	8 slices		pitted olives	to taste
fresh bacon	100 g		pitted black olives	
olive oil	2 dl			

Mix the foie gras with the chopped fresh bacon, the pitted olives
and half of the herbs.
Clean the pheasants well, open and stuff with the foie gras mixture.
Wrap with sliced bacon and tie with string.
Marinate for several hours in the red wine, Port, salt, pepper
and the rest of the herbs.

Slice one onion and sauté until golden and then add pheasants.
Add the marinade, cover and cook for a little while.
Reduce the heat and cook until the pheasants are tender.

Meanwhile, cook the unpeeled potatoes. Peel and sauté until
golden in lard.
Fry one onion in olive oil until soft and add chestnuts. Add sautéed
potatoes and mix.

In a deep serving dish, arrange the potatoes, chestnuts and fried onions.
Place pheasants on top and cover with sauce.

10-year-old Vintage

Loin Fillets of Lamb

wrapped in potato and apple crèpes

loin fillets of lamb	4 (200g each)
apples	4 medium
potatoes	4 medium
butter	2 Tbsp
thyme	to taste
rosemary	to taste
coarse salt	to taste
chopped fresh garlic	1
turnip or collard greens	as required
cooking oil	as required

Trim all the fat from the lamb and season with salt, pepper, thyme and rosemary. Brown in hot oil and reserve.

Peel the potatoes and cut into very think sticks. Peel and grate the apples. Mix well together but do not wash the potatoes so as not to remove the starch.
Heat a non-stick frying pan and make four crèpes. Place the crèpes on grease-proof paper, wrap around each fillet of lamb and bake at 250°C for approximately 15 minutes.

Meanwhile, chop the cooked greens and sauté in olive oil and chopped garlic. In a deep dish place the crèpes and serve with the greens.

10-year-old Vintage

Beef Entrecôte

With deep-fried vegetables and red wine butter

beef entrecôte	4 (180g each)
red wine	2 dl
butter	120 g
onion	1 medium
white wine	1 dl
carrots	as required
string beans	as required
flour	100 g
eggs	2
olive oil	dl

In a pan, add the wine and the chopped onion. Stirring constantly, cook until all the liquid has been reduced. Cool slightly, add softened butter and blend well. Wrap in cling film and place in refrigerator.

Make a batter with flour, beaten egg yolks, white wine and a trickle of olive oil. Beat egg whites until stiff and fold into the batter. Season with salt and pepper.

Cook the vegetables, dip in batter and deep fry. Drain to remove excess fat.

Grill the entrecôtes and place on a serving dish with a slice of wine butter. Arrange vegetables alongside.

Vintage Character or Young LBV

Duck Rice

with layers of vegetables and smokehouse meats

duck	1200 g
smoked pig's ear	1
chouriço (paprika sausage)	1 (100 g)
salpicão (pork and ham sausage)	100g
white cabbage	1 small head
carrots	200 g
rice	240 g
onions	2 medium
egg yolk	1

Soak the pig's ear to remove the salt. Boil the duck, pig's ear, chouriço and salpicão in water seasoned with salt and black pepper. Reserve the stock. Remove the cooked meats and shred, removing all the bones and skin from the duck. Cut the pig's ear into small pieces.

In a pan, fry the chopped onion in olive oil, add the rice and mix well. Add the stock (2 measures of stock for 1 of rice) and adjust the seasonings. Cook over a slow heat until done.

Cook the cabbage and carrots in the stock and drain well.

In a deep ovenproof dish, place a layer of rice, a layer of shredded meats, a layer of vegetables and finish with a layer of rice. Brush with beaten egg yolk and grill in the oven until brown.

Young LBV

Breaded Fillets of Veal

with Island Azores cheese, sautéed greens and potatoes

loin of veal	800 g
grated Ilhas cheese	100 g
breadcrumbs	100 g
eggs	2
turnip or collard greens	300 g
garlic cloves	2
potatoes	400 g
leeks	2
onions	2
lemon	1

Cook the greens in a large pan of salted water. Drain well.
Cook the unpeeled potatoes.
Peel and slice into thin half moons and sauté until golden
in olive oil with crushed garlic. Keep warm.

Cut the loin of veal into thin slices. Hammer until very thin and season
with salt, pepper and lemon juice. Set aside for a few moments and
dredge in flour, beaten egg and lastly in breadcrumbs mixed with
grated cheese. Fry in a little very hot oil
and drain of all fat.

Arrange the greens, sautéed potatoes and breaded fillets on a serving dish.
Garnish with sliced lemon.

Ruby

Pork

with chestnuts and small onions

pork	800 g
peeled raw chestnuts	400 g
potatoes	400 g
fresh mushrooms	200 g
onions	8 very small
white wine	2 dl
garlic cloves	2
bay leaf	2
sweet paprika	1 tsp
olive oil	2 Tbsp
lard	2 Tbsp
rosemary	to taste
ground cumin	to taste

Cut the pork into 2-inch cubes and season with salt, pepper, paprika, one chopped garlic clove. Bay leaves and white wine.

Peel the potatoes, cut into 2-inch cubes and fry in a pan.

Heat the olive oil in a large pan, add the other chopped garlic and the cubed onion.
Simmer a little and add the mushrooms cut in half and the chestnuts.
Cover and simmer a little while longer.

Fry the cubed pork in the lard until brown.
Add the meat and the potatoes to the onions and simmer for a few moments so that all the flavours are well blended.

Serve in a deep dish and sprinkle with rosemary and ground cumin.

Ruby

Loin of Young Beef

toasted with sesame seeds and accompanied by gratinéed potatoes

loin of young veal	800 g		carrots	250 g
potatoes	400 g		turnips	250 g
thick cream	2 dl		grated mild cheese	50 g
milk	2 dl		garlic cloves	2
toasted sesame seeds	as required		nutmeg	to taste
black pepper	to taste		bay leaf	2
butter	1 Tbsp.		sugar	1 level Tbsp

Season the meat with salt and black pepper and dredge well
in sesame seeds.
Brown in a pan and roast at 220°C for about 20 minutes.

Place milk, half of the cream, 1 tablespoon of butter, garlic, bay leaves
and nutmeg. Bring to a boil and add finely sliced potatoes.
Reduce heat and cook until done.

Line the bottom of a shallow ovenproof dish with the potatoes,
removing excess liquid. Cover with cream, sprinkle with
grated cheese and grill in the oven.

Meanwhile, cut the carrots and turnips into cubes or sticks and boil.
Drain and sauté in the butter with the sugar until glazed.

Cut the meat into thick slices and arrange on a platter with the glazed
vegetables. Serve with the gratinéed potatoes.

Vintage Character

Breast of Duck

toasted with honey and soy sauce and accompanied with dry mushroom rice

breasts of duck	4
onion	1 medium
dry mushrooms	100 g
rice	120 g
meat stock	about 2 cups
honey	2 Tbsp
soy souce	4 Tbsp
olive oil	1 dl
cooking oil	2 dl

Soak mushrooms in water for 2 hours, drain and reserve the liquid.
In a pan, heat the olive oil and add the chopped onion. Sauté until golden and add the mushrooms. Cover and simmer for a few minutes. Add the water from the mushrooms and meat stock (double the amount of the rice). Bring to a boil and add rice. Cook over a low heat for 15 minutes.

Season the breasts of duck with salt and black pepper and brown in hot oil.
Brush the meat with honey and sprinkle with soy sauce.
Bake at 250°C for 15 minutes.

Make a bed of rice and arrange the sliced breasts of duck.

20 to 40 Years Old Tawny

Partridge with Grapes

accompanied with spicy vegetable rolls

partridges	4		white wine	2 dl
onions	2		raisins	40 g
carrots	200g		walnut meat	40 g
leeks	200 g		pine nuts	40 g
bacon	100 g		saffron	to taste
flour	200 g		salt	to taste
eggs	2		black pepper	to taste
cooking oil	3 Tbsp		olive oil	as required
melted butter	as required		eggs	2

Place the flour on the table and add just enough water to make a dough.
Add 3 Tbsp of oil, knead well and leave to rest for 2 hours. Roll out on a
pastry cloth and spread out with your hands until it is paper thin.
Cut into rectangles.

In a pan, heat olive oil and fry 1 chopped onion, thinly sliced leeks and
carrots cut into very thin sticks. Add raisins, saffron, salt and black pepper,
bacon, walnuts and pine nuts.

Place a little of this mixture on each rectangle and roll closed.
Place on an ovenproof dish, brush with beaten egg and melted butter.
Bake at 200°C for 15 minutes.

Clean the partridge and season with white wine, salt and pepper.
Brown in hot oil. Add 1 sliced onion and cook in a pressure cooker
for 15 minutes after it has come to the boil.

Place the partridge on a deep serving dish, cover with the sauce
and arrange the vegetable rolls around.

10 to 15-year-old Vintage

Desserts

Pear Tart à la Mode

with raspberry sauce

pears	6 ripe
fresh or frozen raspberries	200 g
flour	150 g
granulated sugar	340 g
egg	1 yolk
butter	40 g
vanilla ice-cream	200 g
lemon juice	to taste
cinnamon	to taste
powdered sugar	to taste

Place the flour on the table and make a well in the middle. In the well, place the egg yolk, 2 tablespoons of water, the butter and the granulated sugar. Mix well, knead and set aside for 2 hours.

Meanwhile, peel the pears and slice lengthwise. Sprinkle with lemon juice to keep them from blackening.

Butter the bottom of a pie pan. Roll the dough out until it is 1 inch thick and line the pie pan.

Arrange the pear slices in overlapping circles in the pie pan and sprinkle With 100 g sugar. Bake at 200°C for 25 minutes.

Meanwhile, put the raspberries and 240 g of sugar in a pan and boil, stirring constantly for 10 minutes. Remove from the heat and cool slightly. Strain through a sieve and place in the refrigerator for a little while.

Pour a little raspberry sauce on the place, a slice of pear tart and a scoop of vanilla ice-cream on the side. Sprinkle with powdered sugar and cinnamon.

40 Years Old Tawny

Melon Sherbert

with red fruit
and almond sticks

melon	600 g
assorted red fruit (red currants, raspberries, strawberries, etc.)	250 g
sugar	625 g
peeled chopped almonds	125 g
flour	125 g
egg	1
water	2 dl
ground toasted almonds	garnish

Peel the melon, remove all the seeds and purée in the electric blender.
Add 200g of sugar and 1 $^1/_2$ dl water.

Place in the ice cream machine and freeze until it gains consistency,
then place in the freezer until just before serving.

In a pan, mix the red fruit with 175 g of sugar and boil for 10 minutes.
Remove from the heat and cool.

Mix the flour and chopped almonds. Add the remaining sugar and the
egg and mix well to form a dough. Make sticks about 1 inch thick,
place on a buttered and lightly-floured cookie sheet and bake
at 250°C for 5 minutes. Cool.

Make a square of almond sticks on the place on which you are going
to servethe sherbert. Place a scoop of sherbert in the centre and pour
the fruit sauce around the whole.

Garnish with ground toasted almonds and powdered sugar.

20 Years Old Tawny

Strawberries

with sabayon sauce
and Portuguese cake biscuits

strawberries	450 g.		**cake**	
egg yolks	2,5 dl.		eggs	5
sugar	6		sugar	125 g.
whipped cream	150 g.		flour	125 g.
white wine	2 dl.			

Cook in a double boiler. In the top pan, place the egg yolks, sugar and white wine. Beat energetically with a whisk until this forms a light and fluffy cream, taking care that the water in the bottom half is always boiling. Remove from the heat, cool and fold whipped cream in very carefully. Keep in a cool place until serving.

Make the cake by beating the whole eggs with the sugar until the eggs have doubled in size.
Sift the flour and add gradually to the eggs, folding it in carefully.
Butter a round mould with a hole in the middle and bake at 200°C in a pre-heated oven For 30 minutes. Cool. Cut into triangular slices and toast them under the grill.

Wash and cut the strawberries into quarters and line the bottom of a dessert cup. Cover with the cream sauce and garnish with slices of the toasted Portuguese cake.

10 Years Old Tawny

Egg Pudding

with pineapple soaked in Port Wine

egg yolks	15
sugar	600 g
fresh pineapple	1
sweet liqueur	1 glass
Port Wine	2 dl
powdered cinnamon	to taste

Mix the egg yolks with the liqueur.
Boil 400g of sugar in 2 dl of water for 4 minutes.
Cook slightly and add egg yolks mixture.

In a small pot, boil 200g of sugar with a little water until it forms
a thin caramel. Coat the inside of a pudding tin with the hot caramel,
cool and add the above egg and sugar mixture.

Place the pudding tin on a tray with sufficient water to cover the tin
half-way. Bake at 150°C for 45 minutes. Cool.

Meanwhile, peel and slice the pineapple and place in a deep bowl.
Cover with Port Wine and leave to soak for 2 hours.

Unmould the pudding and place on a serving dish. Pour any liquid
caramel from the tin over it. Surround with the soaked pineapple pieces.
Sprinkle with cinnamon and garnish with almond sticks.

Old Vintage

Apple and Cinnamon Torte

flaky pastry	400 g
apples	6
egg	1
sugar	100 g
milk	2 dl
cornstarch	1 tsp
powdered cinnamon	1 Tbsp
strawberry jam	2 Tbsp
powdered cinnamon	garnish

Roll the pastry until it forms a rectangle 12 x 5 inch rectangle.
With a sharp knife, mark a rectangle 2 inches from the edge,
taking care not to cut right down to the very bottom.

Peel and slice the apples very finely and layer all over the pastry, within
the borders of the second rectangle. Sprinkle with a little sugar and
cinnamon. Brush the outer rectangle of pastry with beaten egg.
Bake at 250°C for 10 minutes.
Reduce the temperature to 150°C and bake another 20 minutes. Cool.

Meanwhile, make a cinnamon sauce: place the milk, 100 g of sugar
and 1 tablespoon of powdered cinnamon in a pan. Bring to a boil
and add the cornstarch.
Bring again to a boil, remove from the heat and cool.

Pour the cinnamon sauce on the service dish and place a slice of the
apple torte on top. Sprinkle with powdered cinnamon and garnish with
a little strawberry jam.

30 Years Old Tawny

Bread Pudding

with raspberry sauce

milk	1 L
eggs	6
sugar	250 g
bread	150 g
raspberries	200 g
honey	1 Tbsp

Cut the bread into cubes and toast lightly in the oven.
In a pan, mix the milk, sugar and the honey and bring to a boil.
Add the beaten eggs. Butter a loaf tin and dust lightly with sugar.
Line the bottom of the tin with the bread cubes and cover with the
milk mixture. Bake at 150°C for 30 minutes. Cool.

Meanwhile, mix the raspberries and an equal weight of sugar in a pan
and boil for 5 minutes. Strain through a sieve. Keep a few raspberries
aside as a garnish.

Pour the raspberry sauce on a serving dish and place a slice of the
bread pudding on top. Garnish with whole raspberries.

Tawny

Almond Cake

with chocolate and vanilla sauces

Cake			Sauces	
peeled almonds	125 g		sugar	50 g
sweet cooking chocolate	100 g		flour	100 g
eggs	6		thick cream	2 dl
egg yolks	3		butter	50
sugar	250 g		vanilla	1 stick

Chop the almonds very fine in the blender. Add the 6 egg yolks and blend.
Add sugar, flour, lemon peel and melted butter. Mix very well.

Beat the 6 egg whites until stiff and fold in the above mixture.
Place in a buttered and lightly floured cake tin.
Cook at 250°C for 10 minutes.
Reduce the temperature to 150°C and bake another 25 minutes.

Meanwhile, melt the chocolate in a pan. In another pan, bring the cream
to a boil. Remove from the heat and add melted chocolate and mix well.

In a pot, boil milk, sugar and vanilla.

Mix sugar with the egg yolks and the cornstarch. Add to the milk and
bring to a boil until thickened Remove the stick of vanilla and cool.

Pour two spoons of chocolate and two spoons of vanilla sauce on the
serving dish to form an X. With a knife, cut across the two sauces with a
circular movement to make a spiral design. Place a slice of almond cake
on the sauce and sprinkle with powdered sugar.

Young LBV

Tea Pudding

with cinnamon and lemon sticks

Pudding		Biscuits	
sugar	400 g.	flour	150 g
black tea leaves	20 g	sugar	150 g
egg yolks	15	butter	150 g
water	2 dl	honey	100 g
		lemon juice	1 Tbsp
		powdered cinnamon	1 Tbsp

Bring the water to a boil and add the tea leaves. Strain the liquid. Add
sugar and boil for 4 minutes. Remove from heat and add beaten egg yolks.
Make a liquid caramel by boiling 150 g of sugar with 2 Tbsp water.
Coat the inside of a pudding tin with the caramel.
Fill the tin with the mixture, place over a pan with water and bake
at 150°C. For 45 minutes. Cool. To unmould, hold the tin over the fire
for a few seconds.

Meanwhile, make the biscuits.

In a pan, mix butter, honey, lemon juice and cinnamon and heat gently
until the sugar and the butter have melted. Remove from the heat and
add flour. Line a biscuit tray with greaseproof paper and drop large
spoonsfuls of the mixture on the paper. Bake at 200°C for 10 minutes.
Remove from the oven and quickly roll the biscuits into sticks
while still hot.

Place a slice of pudding on a platter and decorate with biscuits.
Garnish with powdered cinnamon and any caramel left in the tin.

Reserve Tawny

Apple Pudding
with fennel sticks

Pudding			Biscuits	
apples	8		flour	150 g.
milk	0,5 l		butter	75 g.
sugar	250 g.		sugar	75 g.
eggs	6		chopped fennel	1
flour	2 Tbsp		molasses	2 Tbsp
cinnamon	1			

Peel the apples and cut into thin slices.
Butter a loaf tin and powder lightly with sugar.
Place the apples in the tin and sprinkle with cinnamon.
Mix the milk with the sugar, flour and eggs and pour over the apples.
Bake over a pan of water at 150°C for 40 minutes. Cool.

Meanwhile, make the biscuits:

Mix all the ingredients and beat well. Shape small biscuits
and bake at 200°C for 10 minutes. Cool.

Place a slice of apple pudding on a plate and surround with biscuits.
Garnish with a sprig of fresh fennel and sprinkle with cinnamon.

Sweet White

Layered Chocolate Biscuit

with fresh fruit

bitter chocolate	250 g.
flour	40 g
sugar	250 g
eggs	6
strawberries	100 g
raspberries	100 g
pineapple	100 g
banana	100 g
thick cream	2 dl
orange liqueur	1 glass
sugar	100 g

Melt the chocolate in a double boiler or in the microwave oven.
Aside, beat the egg yolks well with the sugar.
Add the flour and mix well.
Add the melted chocolate. Gently fold in the egg whites beaten stiff.

Line a biscuit tray with greaseproof paper and bake at 200°C for
15 minutes. Cool and cut into small 2 x 4 inch rectangles.

Peel and slice the fruit, leaving the raspberries whole.
Whip the cream with the sugar and blend in the orange liqueur.

Place a rectangle of biscuit on a serving dish. With a icing tube, spread a
little cream and place some fruit. Cover with another rectangle and
repeat the cream and fruit. Top with a biscuit rectangle. Sprinkle
powdered sugar and garnish with remaining fruit.

10 to 20-year-old Vintage

Hazlenut Cake

with chickpea cream

Cake	
flour	100 g
sugar	150 g
eggs	6
grated hazlenuts	75 g
Cream	
dry chickpeas	250 g
sugar	200 g
egg yolks	6
Water	1 dl

Soak the chickpeas for several hours or overnight.
Beat the eggs with the sugar until double in volume.
Carefully fold in the flour and the grated almonds.
Butter and lightly flour a rectangular cake tin and fill.
Cook at 200°C for 30 minutes.

Meanwhile, cook the chickpeas in a pressure cooker for 15 minutes
beginnng when they come to a boil. Drain and purée.
In a pan, boil the sugar with 1 dl of water.
5 minutes after it has come to a boil,
add the puréed chickpeas. Mix well and add the egg yolks and cook,
stirring constantly until the cream begins to become stiff. (It is ready
when you cross it with a knife or a spoon and the sides stay standing.)

Slice the cake in half and cover the bottom half with the cream.
Cover with the other half. Sprinkle with powdered sugar
and grated hazlenuts.

30 Years Old Tawny

Sweet Marrow

and Almond Cake

drained sweet marrow preserve	150 g
ground almonds	100 g
eggs	6
flour	100 g
sugar	250 g
butter	250 g

Beat the butter and the sugar until creamy. Add the egg yolks, almonds, the marrow preserve, the flour and lastly, the egg whites beaten stiff.
Butter and lightly flour a round cake tin.
Bake at 200°C for 45 minutes.

Sprinkle with powdered sugar and toasted almonds just before serving.

Dry White

Pineapple Sherbert

with cottage cheese pasties

Sherbert	
pineapple	400 g
sugar	250 g
water	2 dl
Pasties	
sugar	200 g
egg yolks	8
flaky pastry	packet
powdered cinnamon	garnish
ground hazlenuts	garnish

Sherbert: Boil the sugar and the water for 2 minutes. Purée the pineapple and add to the sugar. Bring again to a boil and cook for 4 minutes. Cool and beat in the ice cream machine until creamy. Remove and keep in a cool place.

Pasties: Roll out the pastry and line the pasty tins. Mix the cottage cheese with the sugar and egg yolks. Fill the pasty tins and bake at 200°C for 20 minutes.

On a dish, arrange a pasty next to a scoop of pineapple sherbert. Sprinkle with powdered cinnamon and ground hazlenuts.

Sweet White

Strawberry Mille-Feuilles

with orange cream

fresh strawberries	400 g
flaky pastry	400 g
eggs	3
milk	2 dl
sugar	200 gr
cornstarch	1 tsp
thick cream	2 dl
Cointreau	1 glass
grated orange peel	1 orange

Roll out the pastry and shape two 8 x 4 inch rectangles.
Brush with 1 beaten egg and bake at 250°C for 10 minutes.
Reduce temperature to 150°C and bake until the pastry is dry.

Bring the milk to boil in a pot. Aside, blend 2 egg yolks with the sugar
and cornstarch. Mix well and add to hot milk.
Cook until thickened. Cool.
Whip the cream and add to the cool sauce. Gently fold in the Cointreau
and the grated orange peel until well blended.

Wash the strawberries and slice thinly. Mix with the cream.

Open the pastry rectangles to form 4 sheets. Fill these sheets with the
strawberry cream. Cut into smaller pieces. Place on a serving dish and
garnish with uncut fresh strawberries.

40 Years Old Tawny

Caramel Custard

with apples

milk	1 l
egg yolks	8
sugar	400 g
cornstarch	2 Tbsp
apples	6 medium
powdered cinnamon	1 tsp
butter	1 Tbsp
lemon peel	1 twist

Peel and quarter the apples. Cook covered over a low heat with 100 g
of sugar and the butter until creamy. Add cinnamon and pour
into a deep dish.

Bring the milk and lemon peel to a boil.
Aside, mix egg yolks, remaining sugar and cornstarch. Slowly add the
hot milk, stirring constantly, and cook until thickened.

Pour the custard over the apples and cool slightly.
Sprinkle well with granulated sugar and caramelise the sugar
with a hot iron.

20 Years Old Tawny

Acknowlegments

Porto Palácio Hotel
César Castro Lda
Afonso Soares
Adozinda Gonçalves
João Pereira
Drª Sónia Botelho
Srº Claudio Canú
Drª Ana Maria Brochado Coelho

Title

Recipies to Accompany Port Wine

Author

Hélio Loureiro

Wine Selection

Alfredo Hervias Mendizabal
João Nicolau de Almeida
Miguel Castro Silva

Editors

Instituto do Vinho do Porto
Campo das Letras

Produced by

João Machado Design Lda

Translation

Magdalena Gorrell Guimaraens

Design

João Machado

Photographs

João Paulo Sottomayor

Date of Edition

March, 2000

Draft Printing

Loja das Ideias

Printers

Norprint

Legal Depository

149358/00

ISBN

972-610-207-3